THE MAP OF CLAY

by the same author

WILDING GRAFT

CONFESSION OF A REBEL

THE INVADING GOSPEL

The portrait of Jack Clemo reproduced
as the frontispiece is from an oil
painting by Lionel Miskin, to whom our
thanks are due for permission to use it

The Map of Clay

by
Jack Clemo

with an Introduction by
CHARLES CAUSLEY

METHUEN · LONDON

The Map of Clay first published in 1961
by Methuen & Co. Ltd., 36 Essex Street, WC2
© 1961 by Jack Clemo
'The Clay Verge' was originally published
by Chatto & Windus in 1951. 'The Wintry
Priesthood' won a prize in the Arts Council
Festival of Britain Competition and was
included in the Penguin anthology *Poems 1951*.
Printed in Great Britain by
The Camelot Press Ltd., London & Southampton
Catalogue No. 2/6405/1

CONTENTS

FRONTIER SIGNALS

THE WORLD OF JACK CLEMO

Jack Clemo still lives in the four-roomed, slate-roofed granite box of a cottage on Goonamarris Slip in which he was born in 1916: in a hamlet seven miles north-west of St Austell, lodged deep in the gut of the Cornish china-clay industry.

Here is the lunar and lunatic landscape of the moon: a weird, white world dusted over with the colour of sex, where the workers are like walking wedding cakes. Great claypits have yawned and swallowed lovers' paths, fields, farms, farm-buildings and sometimes each other. Stalking sand-burrows, green-grown pyramids of mica, squat at the back doors of houses as if waiting to edge them over. And the water at the bottom of the deep, abandoned pits looks up at the sky and the stabbing eye with a flat, pale, powdery, blind, blue stare.

Clemo's father was an illiterate clay-worker, a "dry" man who worked in the kilns. He joined the Royal Navy as a stoker in the First World War and was lost at the age of twenty-seven off the Dutch coast in the destroyer *Tornado*. But the death of Reginald Clemo was only one of a succession of blows that was to hammer his wife and her only surviving child: a single instance in a chain of events that the poet, long after, was able to describe as

7

The motions of that twisted, dark,
Deliberate crucial Will
I feel deep-grinding still
Under the dripping clay with which I am baptized.

In his savagely brilliant autobiography *Confession of a Rebel*,[1] Jack Clemo writes of that remarkable woman his mother at about this time, foreseeing the coming years as Tess Durbeyfield saw her tomorrows, "very fierce and cruel, as if they would say, 'I'm coming. Beware of me! Beware of me!' "

At the age of five, Clemo suffered his first attack of blindness. This lasted five months, and its terrors, at that particular time and place, transformed him from a plump, pink, chattering boy into a "thin, pasty-faced brat, dull-eyed, silent and morbid". At thirteen, his sight failed again for three months and Clemo's formal education came to an end. In any case, like many another artist, the child – with his passionate love of solitary brooding – loathed school, and "never really came under its grip at all".

But his blazing and unlikely desire was to be a creative writer, and he began to hack his novels and poems from the "landscape of purgation" that surrounded him. At eighteen, his hearing began to show signs of damage, and he has remained stone-deaf for much of his adult life. And his lack of success as a novelist over the first twenty years of his output can only be described as scintillating. Before the critical acclaim for his first published novel *Wilding Graft*[2] in

[1] Chatto & Windus (1949)   [2] Chatto & Windus (1948)

1948, he wrote a dozen or so others: every one a failure.

In 1955, blindness returned and has largely prevented him continuing with his prose work, though he was able to produce in 1958 *The Invading Gospel*:[1] a statement of religious philosophy that also throws a strong and striking light on the imagery and intellectual climate of his verse. And, since darkness set in again, he has continued with his verse: the supreme and sharpest achievement, I believe, in the four-pronged thrust of his work as a novelist, autobiographer, philosopher and poet.

What is it, in the teeth of disasters and discouragements that would have destroyed a lesser man, that makes Clemo tick? The answer, quite simply, is that he has always regarded his afflictions as a test of faith. I remember vividly how he spoke drily to me once of himself as a clay phoenix, continually experiencing "all this singeing of feathers mythical and mystical birds have to go through".

Reading the first group of poems that follow, it is important to remember Clemo's sternly uncompromising Calvinism, his acceptance of the doctrine of Election, his recognition of the possibility that if a man wears on his brow the badge of salvation, God will hunt him down, imprison him if necessary in every kind of jail of the flesh. In this way, finally, Clemo believes grace descends – in the vision of George Herbert – as "thy silk twist let down from Heaven to me".

[1] Geoffrey Bles (1958)

9

The dominant theme of much of Clemo's verse is the relationship of religion and sex: the word "priest" clearly used in Browning's sense of "priest and lover". And the last section of poems here collected is written, Clemo emphasizes, as a "revivalist jazz crescendo celebrating the sense of release from a tragic, Hardyesque fate".

Clemo has a livid and lively horror of being regarded, because of his physical handicaps, as some kind of literary freak or as a pathetic wreck of a man deserving only pity. For myself, I can only say that the significance and power of his writings have always rendered quite incidental, irrelevant, the appalling difficulties under which he works. Nevertheless, he admits bluntly in his autobiography, "I am one of those writers whose creative work cannot be *fully*[1] understood without reference to certain broken boundaries in their private lives."

By what he would call a miracle, and certainly in the face of medical evidence to the contrary, Clemo has more than once regained his faculties.[2] He believes that this will happen again, and refuses resolutely, for example, to learn Braille. To adopt the apparatus of a blind man would seem to him a collapse of faith. At present, his chief means of communication with the outside world is through his sixty-six-year-old mother, a determined Methodist of equally formidable faith,

[1] My italics.
[2] By the end of 1956 Clemo's hearing had partially returned, and he has had no subsequent relapse. He is able to detect various sounds around him and to enjoy music on records and radio, though speech remains unintelligible.

who is able to talk to him by tracing block letters of the alphabet with her finger on the palm of his hand.

Sitting in the Clemos' kitchen, by the china dogs and the honeysuckle tiles on the grate, the photographs of Billy Graham and T. F. Powys, the glass-fronted bookcase with its volumes of Spurgeon and D. H. Lawrence, Karl Barth and Coventry Patmore, the Browning love-letters and the Picasso reproductions, I have never found myself in a hermetically-sealed hermit's cell. Incredibly, to the outsider, it is a home of happiness and hope.

Jack Clemo once described himself as the oddest writer Cornwall ever produced. I would describe him as one of the greatest. Whether I have been with him in the cottage on Goonamarris Slip, or re-reading his poems in my own Cornish home on the other side of the great frozen sea of Bodmin Moor, I have never doubted that I am in the presence of a man whose make-up includes genius.

CHARLES CAUSLEY

The Clay Verge

A CALVINIST IN LOVE

I will not kiss you, country fashion,
    By hedgesides where
    Weasel and hare
Claim kinship with our passion.

I care no more for fickle moonlight:
    Would rather see
    Your face touch me
Under a claywork dune-light.

I want no scent or softness round us
    When we embrace:
    We could not trace
Therein what beauties bound us.

This bare clay-pit is truest setting
    For love like ours:
    No bed of flowers
But sand-ledge for our petting.

The Spring is not our mating season:
    The lift of sap
    Would but entrap
Our souls and lead to treason.

This truculent gale, this pang of winter
    Awake our joy,
    For they employ
Moods that made Calvary splinter.

We need no vague and dreamy fancies:
          Care not to sight
          The Infinite
In transient necromancies.

No poetry on earth can fasten
          Its vampire mouth
          Upon our youth:
We know the sly assassin.

We cannot fuse with fallen Nature's
          Our rhythmic tide:
          It is allied
With laws beyond the creatures.

It draws from older, sterner oceans
          Its sensuous swell:
          Too near to Hell
Are we for earthly motions.

Our love is full-grown Dogma's offspring,
          Election's child,
          Making the wild
Heats of our blood an offering.

THE WATER-WHEEL

Dead wood with its load of stones
          Amid the living wood!
Tugged by the wheel the ballast groans,
          Casts on the little brood
          Of trees its alien mood.

The wheel spins dourly round,
  Wet flanges menacing,
Yet curbed and forced back underground,
  Snarling and shuddering
  Beneath the water's sting.

The iron rods are gripped;
  Tree-high the pulleys slur:
The budding boughs are bruised and stripped:
  Dead iron, live branches blur
  In rhythmic massacre.

The plashy ground turns white
  With clay-silt from the wheel,
And still the trough pours on to smite
  Both wood and iron, to seal
  The dream-world with the real.

PRISONER OF GOD

Who needs forgiveness now?
For You had prisoned me
Within the walls of pain-dark mystery,
And left her free to vow
Her life to other ends and so escape
These damps You chose for me, this mould and grime
Which fashions me for monkhood, not the slime
In honest daylight of the hungering clay.
That was her choice, and somebody must pay.

Why should it not be You
Who tore our fates apart and broke the shape
And pattern of the dual stress
Matching the mightiness
Of that articulation I deemed true,
That Word which braves all prisons, bids rejoice?
You would not hear my voice,
And how could I hear Yours
When You were slamming, slamming all my doors?
You spurned my inner light,
And how could I reveal
Such rays as faith afforded of the bright
Christ-essence when Your hand
Was resolute to seal
The windows of my tower through which I scanned
The vain horizons for a trace
Of her returning form? There was no place
For common measurements of sin:
And why did You begin
This wasteful loss of Your own Self in me?
Why foolishly redeem
If with redemption comes the shattered dream
Of human joys which she
Gains without prayer or vision? Why elate
Upon that Easter turret of Your power
When I am buried still in His dark hour
And *her* heaven mocks us both? You know this state
Of infinite wreckage sprung
From trustful heart and glad obedient tongue.

When in the courtyard the world's hammers rang,
Driving the nails for greed
Of faithless fleshly meed
And coarsest earthly tang,
I was apart with her and for relief
Of that sore martyrdom, even though belief
Flamed in our kisses, not in altar smoke,
And these dark corridors awoke
To other genuflections than are used
In churches where His truth is bruised
By scholarship or art.
You set us there to start
The blood's crusade against all doubt of Him,
And yet maliciously
Barred off her blood from faith which grew to me
More beautiful than her own body till
She felt His breath in mine; and then the dim
Sick transformation crept through nerves and will,
And my long destined night
Closed, following her flight:
And Your almighty ban
Forestalled my every plan
To reach her heaven or His.
With tasteless ironies
You fill my days for me, this only life
Which has no choice but has surrendered all
In trust that through the strife
By which I died in Him the Fall
Would cease to live in her.
What grace do You confer

Through tricks like these? What love could shape such
    doom?
These are my facts. What shall my verdict be,
Baptized into such sonship, when this gloom
Breaks at Christ's Judgment-seat which sets me free?

NEUTRAL GROUND

God's image was washed out of Nature
    By the flood of the Fall:
No symbol remains to inspire me,
    And none to appal.

His Hand did not fashion the vistas
    These poets admire,
For He is too busied in glutting
    The worm and the fire.

Not in Nature or God must my vision
    Now find some relief
While I deepen my hatred of beauty,
    Suspend my belief.

I will turn to a world that is ravaged,
    Yet not by His Will,
A world whose derision of Nature
    Is rigid and shrill.

I have lost all the sensitive, tender,
    Deep insights of man:
I will look round a claywork in winter,
    And note what I can.

SNOWFALL AT KERNICK

Here with a burly flutter and sting
  The snow-blast scampers winnowing,
And dribble of foam-flakes seeps and bores
  Through clay-clump thickets, under doors;
While flurry of snow-mist rises where
  The waggons tug till rails are bare.
The smoke is battered round the stacks;
  Soot falls with snow on trolley-tracks.
Even the mica-channel planks
  And narrow walls of settling-tanks
Are frilled and ice-splashed there between
  The frozen pools now sickly green.
The pit-edge merges with the fields,
  A softened gash the clay-bone shields;
Beyond it in the valley's fold
  Virginia woods loom taut and cold.

THE FLOODED CLAY-PIT

    These white crags
  Cup waves that rub more greedily
  Now half-way up the chasm; you see
    Doomed foliage hang like rags;
    The whole clay-belly sags.

    What scenes far
  Beneath those waters: chimney-pots
  That used to smoke; brown rusty clots
    Of wheels still oozing tar;
    Lodge doors that rot ajar.

Those iron rails
Emerge like claws cut short on the dump,
Though once they bore the waggon's thump:
    Now only toads and snails
    Creep round their loosened nails.

Those thin tips
Of massive pit-bed pillars – how
They strain to scab the pool's face now,
    Pressing like famished lips
    Which dread the cold eclipse.

THE CINDER-HEAP

For twenty years they have lain,
Scorned by the sun and nudged by wind and rain,
Flaky and brittle scabs on mouldering sand.
The whole dune-face is wrinkled with the bruise
Where ash and gravel interfuse,
And the dim clay-land
Cowers in vague watchfulness and fear
As brambles straggle clear,
Pushing with live brown claws
From the hard refuse through the crust
Thrown out by fires long dead: thick rust
Lies on the furnace there
Where the sagging dune-top draws
Slowly around the roofless walls
Of the old engine-house which falls
More ruinous and bare

With every storm that batters. All that's left
Of purging and consuming fire now feeds
The rousing seeds;
And the world of refuse feels the alien sting
In the crumpled cleft,
In the warmth of Spring:
Sap forcing out through rubble, filming green
With soft coarse leaves the gritty silt
Which pit and engine-house have vainly spilt
To make the earth unclean.
And surly in its bafflement
The old black cinder-heap
Confronts the newer dunes on which no brambles creep,
Though they, too, just as bitterly are bent.
This clay-land of the cleansing jet,
The purging fire,
So fears the living sap, the flamy fret
Through stem and vein of earth's desire.

QUARRY SNOW

There is no beauty in snow on trees
    Compared with the pattern of flakes on these
Angular pit-growths hewn by blast,
    Feathery rock of trunks that cast
Strange corded branches, loops of wire,
Over the gorge-drops. I desire
No glimpse of flower-cups smirking through
    Snow fettered fields – would rather view
The quarry's yield: a lone crowbar,
    A pulley-frame, a can of tar,

Wheelbarrows soft in puffy gloom,
 Or trolley-rope's cold flaky plume,
A waggon-track with white ribbed prongs
 Spanning a crevice: here belongs,
In these weird aisles of ghostly stone,
 Humility of symbols' bone.

THE BURNT BUSH

A bush was on that dump:
A single stain of green and gold
'Mid glacial whiteness fold on fold –
A fang of Nature from the cold
And clay-purged sand: denied a clump,
 She put forth one gorse-stump.

I climbed there with a girl:
We squatted in the cleft to watch
The clay-land shadows till a snatch
Of fun led her to strike a match
And set it to the twigs. A curl
 Of crackling flame, a swirl

Of smoke, and we were penned
Behind a knot of fire which licked
Along the bristly stems and flicked
Petals and thorns as ash that pricked
White gravel far below the bend
 We waited to descend.

The clay-face soon was bare.
A few charred twigs remained to show
That Nature's vein was dried: a slow
Thin pulse of smoke trailed in the glow
Of sunset as we climbed with care
    Down to the fresher air.

    Fresh too was my desire.
I looked upon her laughing play
There in the gully's winding way:
A dry cool breeze had bared her clay.
Rain fosters sap and fashions mire,
    But dry clay prompts the fire.

    She fired the gorse – fired too
One gnarled old bush of Adam's seed
Which in a cleft of naked need
Within my soul had fouled indeed
White purity, and as it grew
    Spread doubts in scent and hue.

    Her hand held mine – and then
The flame leapt in and burnt the bush:
My soul knew smoke and fire, then hush
Of clay delivered from the push
Of Nature's sap: now in God's ken
    I stand unsoiled again.

THE PLUNDERED FUCHSIAS

They lie all round the lawn
And on the furrowed wall
Like little red bombs winged and splayed.
No gale has made them fall:
A child's whim, that is all.

She plucked one from the bough
And squeezed the calyx, nipped
Till up welled honey – one clear drop
'Mid pistil-shafts blue-tipped.
Next moment they were ripped

Greedily out and flung
Across the garden while,
The petals underneath her tongue
Pressed backward, she made trial
Of nectar; then her smile

Lit up; sweet vandal hands
Pillaged more blooms, stripped bare
A whole branch in a wasteful freak.
For once she did not care
That a flower's face could be fair.

In those moments she was mine,
The love of beauty's dress
Dead in her eyes, her fingers numbed
From pity or caress
Of Nature's loveliness.

Dear God, but it was heaven
            To see her red lips meet
Those petals with no kiss but glib
            Destructive glee, and cheat
            The bees of their stored sweet.

She marred the rhythm of soil,
            She checked fertility,
And then, the last flower trampled on,
            She turned more naughtily
            And gave her lips to me.

Alone and trembling I
            Stoop now, but not with fear:
These pistils cannot stab my faith:
            Each is a limp spear
            That withers as I peer.

The flower-shells strewn to die,
            Dismantled by her lips,
Were drained where my new life has fed,
            The life that only grips
            Where Nature's in eclipse.

THE CHILD TRAITOR

This too breaks down and has become a snare:
These gambols in the child-world and the rare
Sweet insights unforbidden
Are suddenly all hidden
And crumbled to the old grey-toned despair.

Here as in woman's love a serpent steals,
Breaking the fellowship; her innocence conceals,
And chance now brings to view
The fatal bias – blind urge to embrace
Riot of tidal colour spawned by the sap's race.
I am left desolate, though we were friends;
The flaw again is recognized,
And this companionship I prized
As God's dear whim of mercy ends
In sick betrayal too.

She has turned from God and me
To pluck a foxglove tenderly,
And pressing through the brambles snapped
The thick green stem, fondling the purple bells,
Not feeling the ripe hells
That glow in each for me, who yesterday was lapped
With joy to think my sympathy
Fused with her soul and moving with its tide,
Apart from Nature's teeming perfidies,
Untricked by that false guide.

Each thorn among those blackberries
Has pierced the Hand that made it, yet she loves,
Most plainly loves each little tugging spike,
And witlessly approves
Its freak – unhooks it gently; and were I to strike,
Cutting it dead, or wrest the foxglove flowers,
Trampling them underfoot to thwart the bees
That press old snares upon my mind,
Nuzzling for nectar they could find
In the white feathery womb beneath the velvet towers –

Were I thus to make
A gesture of the way my faith must take,
Her eyes would turn in quick dark mutiny
Of protest, loyal to the staining beauty
And not to God's grey truth that spurred my act.
She cannot understand: she feels at peace,
Child of the earth with ties she cares not to retract.
Where shall I find release?
What world can this raw vision consecrate?
Cast out from child-love as from woman's dower,
I have no friends but things inanimate,
And taste no mood of God save Dogma's power.

CHRIST IN THE CLAY-PIT

Why should I find Him here
And not in a church, nor yet
Where Nature heaves a breast like Olivet
Against the stars? I peer
Upon His footsteps in this quarried mud;
I see His blood
In rusty stains on pit-props, waggon-frames
Bristling with nails, not leaves. There were no leaves
Upon His chosen Tree,
No parasitic flowering over shames
Of Eden's primal infidelity.

Just splintered wood and nails
Were fairest blossoming for Him Who speaks
Where mica-silt outbreaks

29

Like water from the side of His own clay
In that strange day
When He was pierced. Here still the earth-face pales
And rends in earthquake roarings of a blast
With tainted rock outcast
While fields and woods lie dreaming yet of peace
'Twixt God and His creation, of release
From potent wrath – a faith that waxes bold
In churches nestling snugly in the fold
Of scented hillsides where mild shadows brood.
The dark and stubborn mood
Of Him Whose feet are bare upon this mire,
And in the furnace fire
Which hardens all the clay that has escaped,
Would not be understood
By worshippers of beauty toned and shaped
To flower or hymn. I know their facile praise
False to the heart of me, which like this pit
Must still be disembowelled of Nature's stain,
And rendered fit
By violent mouldings through the tunnelled ways
Of all He would regain.

THE EXCAVATOR

I stand here musing in the rain
This Sabbath evening where the pit-head stain
Of bushes is uprooted, strewn
In waggon-tracks and puddles,
While the fleering downpour fuddles

The few raw flowers along the mouldering dump –
Ridge hollowed and rough-hewn
By the daily grind and thump
Of this grim excavator. It shields me
From lateral rain-gusts, its square body turned
To storm-lashed precipices it has churned.

I feel exultantly
The drip of clayey water from the poised
Still bar above me; thrilling with the rite
Of baptism all my own,
Acknowledging the might
Of God's great arm alone;
Needing no ritual voiced
In speech or earthly idiom to draw
My soul to His new law.

The bars now hinged o'erhead and drooping form
A Cross that lacks the symmetry
Of those in churches, but is more
Like His Whose stooping tore
The vitals from our world's foul secrecy.
This too has power to worm
The entrails from a flint, bearing the scoop
With every searching swoop:
That broken-mouthed gargoyle
Whose iron jaws bite the soil,
Snapping with sadist kisses in the soft
White breasts of rocks, and ripping the sleek belly
Of sprawling clay-mounds, lifting as pounded jelly

Flower-roots and bush-tufts with the reeking sand.
I fondle and understand
In lonely worship this malicious tool.

Yes, this is Christian art
To me men could not school
With delicate aesthetes. Their symbols oft
Tempt simple souls like me
Whom Nature meant to seal
With doom of poetry,
And dowered with eye and brain
Sensitive to the stain
Of Beauty and the grace of man's Ideal.
But I have pressed my way
Past all their barren play
Of intellect, adulthood, the refined
Progressive sickness of the mind
Which throws up hues and shapes alien to God's
Way with a man in a stripped clay desert. Now
I am a child again,
With a child's derision of the mentors' rods
And a child's quick pain,
Loving to stand as now in outlawed glee
Amid the squelching mud and make a vow
With joy no priest or poet takes from me.

I cannot speak their language; I am one
Who feels the doggerel of Heaven
Purge earth of poetry; God's foolishness
Laugh through the web man's ripening wisdom spun;
The world's whole culture riven
By moody excavations Love shall bless.

All staining rhythms of Art and Nature break
Within my mind, turn grey, grow truth
Rigid and ominous as this engine's tooth.
And so I am awake:
No more a man who sees
Colour in flowers or hears from birds a song,
Or dares to worship where the throng
Seek Beauty and its old idolatries.
No altar soils my vision with a lax
Adult appeal to sense,
Or festering harmonies' magniloquence.
My faith and symbol shall be stark.
My hand upon these caterpillar-tracks
Bogged in the mud and clay,
I find it easier to pray:
"Keep far from me all loveliness, O God,
And let me laud
Thy meaner moods, so long unprized;
The motions of that twisted, dark,
Deliberate crucial Will
I feel deep-grinding still
Under the dripping clay with which I am baptized."

THE CLAY-TIP WORKER

Our clay-dumps are converging on the land:
Each day a few more flowers are killed,
A few more mossy hollows filled
With gravel. Like a clutching hand

The refuse moves against the dower,
The flaunting pride and power
Of springtide beauty menacing the sod;
And it is joy to me
To lengthen thus a finger of God
That wars with Poetry.

I feel myself a priest,
Crusading from the tip-beams with my load
And pushing out along the iron lines
My gritty symbol of His new designs.
Creation's mood has ceased
Upon this ribbed height; here He has bestowed
Redemptive vision: I advance to pour
Sand, mud and rock upon the store
Of springtime loveliness idolaters adore.

The tarred rope winds across the mead,
Among the bushes and the weed,
Straight over grooved wheels from the sand-cone's
    ridge,
Back to the engine-house beside the bridge.
I watch it draw the waggon up the rails,
Smack the surrounding foliage as it whirrs,
Daubing the ferns and furze
Till they droop black and battered, oily flails
Windblown against the turning spokes
Which catch and mangle frond and blossom, bend them
    over,
Spinning the puffy heads of clover
In dying blobs around the pulley-frames.

And here my faith acclaims
The righting of a balance, a full peace
Slipping from Nature's yokes,
Redemptive truth grey doctrines can release.

This sand-dump's base now licks a hedge
Whose snaky bramble-growths will bear
No flowers or fruit again; a few more days
And they'll be buried 'neath the wedge
Of settling gravel, rotting where
No naturalist may pry to mark their sleep.
The vomit then will creep
Up the sleek boughs of thorn trees that enwrap
The hedge-top, wound and smother them
Till splintered, jammed, they disappear, their sap
Bleeding and drying in the tomb I raise
High over root and soil and mouldering stem.

I love to see the sand I tip
Muzzle the grass and burst the daisy heads.
I watch the hard waves lapping out to still
The soil's rhythm for ever, and I thrill
With solitary song upon my lip,
Exulting as the refuse spreads:
"Praise God, the earth is maimed,
And there will be no daisies in that field
Next spring; it will not yield
A single bloom or grass blade: I shall see
In symbol potently
Christ's Kingdom there restored:
One patch of Poetry reclaimed
By Dogma: one more triumph for our Lord."

THE IRONY OF ELECTION

In that Garden we so sadly name
The trees betrayed Him before Judas came;
And every tree's a Judas still;
Each little flower is glib to fill
The cup of which He prayed:
"Father, may this cup pass."
His memory did not turn towards the grass,
To grape-vine's colour or to cedar's shade:
It sought a city street,
Palms torn and muddied 'neath the ass's feet
And the exultant shout:
"The very stones cry out."
He looked around Gethsemane
And thought: "The streets have been more kind to Me.
The streets were thrilled, but the groves are numb;
The stones cry out, but the flowers die dumb."

In this world of mingled rock and flowers
Wherein the Master plies deific powers
And moodily reveals a Plan
Ripened beyond that Garden's ban,
You see the self-same law
Shatter the rational flaw,
The poet's fancies, even religion's dream.
For when in lonely might His mercies stream
Into our natural sphere,
Or when His noontide burns divinely clear
Above our midnight's heat –
When His triumph is complete,

When He paces our disrupted shore,
Bidding His Kingdom integrate once more,
The foolish thrill, but the wise are numb;
The stones cry out, but the flowers die dumb.

THE WINDS

There is a tree grows upside down,
    Its roots are in the sky;
Its lower branches reach the earth
    When amorous winds are nigh.

On one lone bough there starkly hangs
    A Man just crucified,
And all the other branches bear
    The choice fruits of the Bride.

When Pleasure's wind goes frisking past,
    Unhallowed by a prayer,
It swirls dead leaves from earth-born trees,
    Old growths of pride and care.

The gracious fruits are hidden by
    These leaves of human stain;
The Crucified beneath His load
    Shudders, as if in pain.

But swift springs down a credal wind,
    It thrills through all the boughs;
The dead leaves scatter and are lost;
    The Christ renews His vows.

His hands direct the Spirit's wind
    Branch after branch to shake;
The Bride's fruit drops, and at the touch
    Elected hearts awake.

SUFFICIENCY

Yes, I might well grow tired
Of slighting flowers all day long,
Of making my song
Of the mud in the kiln, of the wired
Poles on the clay-dump; but where
Should I find my personal pulse of prayer
If I turned from the broken, scarred
And unkempt land, the hard
Contours of dogma, colourless hills?
Is there a flower that thrills
Like frayed rope? Is there grass
That cools like gravel, and are there streams
Which murmur as clay-silt does that Christ redeems?
I have not heard of any, so I trace
The writings on bruised iron and purged clay face:
"Young son of man, be strong,
For as My dower is, so shall be your song.
There is no weariness for you,
For I will let you view
In a human flower the soft warm growth:
Her tidal sap has touched the soil of both
The real worlds that you scan,
And thus shall make you man.
In the heights you shall hymn but Godhead grim and grey;
In the depths you shall hymn but clay."

The Wintry Priesthood

A POETIC SEQUENCE

CORNISH ANCHORITE

Deep in the clay-land winter lies my brain,
All faculties that human growth could stain
Dissolved to weedless nescience: here is soil
No poet's pen can scratch, no culture's light despoil.
This vein beyond sap's reach
Teems with no beauties that can teach
My senses mortal joy or mortal pain.
I am exempt at last,
In Dogma's fold till Nature's rhythm be overpast.
I feel a truth the ironic Word has sown,
Truth that draws fibre of human knowledge back
To grey agnostic bone,
Breaks down the nerve of natural piety
To its foul core, turns slack
The muscle of bold self-sufficiency,
And lets the once proud clay
In dumb humility decay.
There is no worship here, only the worm I call
Original sin, and fire of the Fall.
Worm and fire at my roots, how should I know
Your sunshine, song of your birds, you poet brood?
How should I share your pagan glow?
I am beyond your seasons: food
For these is in your blood but not in me.
I lapse from Nature towards a birth
Of Heaven's fertility
That blasphemes Spring upon your earth.

THE BROAD WINTER
(TO C. H. SPURGEON)

What isolates me here in frozen clay
But that same tidal shock which fell
First upon England in your day?
Betrayal of the truth is no new thing
Within the fellowship of Christ, yet new
Was the cold glare whence alien ripples flashed;
New was the odour of that sea, the sting
Of science seeping through
The mass mind of a nation till it dashed
Among the rocks of faith's high Citadel,
The sacramental pass
That guarded rich fields of the heavenly corn.
And the husbandmen, the sworn
Defenders of the mystery – ah, too well
You knew the glib decisions reached,
The furtive codes that circled as
The schooled pen stabbed, the dam was breached,
And your voice thundered amid the rocks
As you strove at the barrier, bearing the central shocks:
"Woe to the idol shepherds who feed not
The sheep, but speak in swelling words
Of human wisdom! Vengence is the Lord's."

The salt taste of that foaming infidelity
Stayed on your lip, the hot
Fever devoured the wounded frame
As in the dire eclipse you lay
There at Menton, the sweet west bay

That smiled on you in hours of kindlier fame.
But now it is evening and mid-winter, cold
With snowy blasts from the Alps, the sea;
And biting to the bone
The bleaker vistas over that dim wave
Which shudders in the memory.

The darkness comes as you foretold.
You hear the fretful moan,
The alien winds that rave
As bitterly the grey truth breaks
On disillusioned Church and frantic world.
You see what form the judgement takes,
What harvest faithless generations reap:
The folds half empty, no clean pasture for the sheep;
Soil sterile where the liberal waters swirled
Which now have hardened into mud
Of festering ethic; fruitless hands grown chill
With their starved, pallid blood;
And the sky freezing still.

When I saw this I chose to dwell
With torturing symbols of the Citadel.

CLAY-LAND MOODS

There squats amid these pyramids
The Sphinx-mood of a Deity,
Unfelt until He bids
Sandstorms awaken and the choking dust
Drive me across the moors of barren trust.

43

Then I perceive the aloof grey shape, the scorn,
Quiet veiled cruelty of the watching eyes:
The grim mysterious Will all help denies.
The feet press out until my roots are torn,
Caught by the mauling claws. In silence He
        Smothers and tortures me.

    Here on the sharp clay-tip there broods
    Olympian thunder, bold and swift,
       Fiercest of all God's moods.
One flash therefrom and peaks of vision seethe
With hostile potency: while wrathful vapours writhe
I creep down rain-grooves, cravenly slink to hide
In caves of the pit, and bruised with panic prayer
Unknown to Mammon's sober workmen there,
I wait till lightnings, thunder-rasps have died
And God allows His terror-mood to lift
       From off the senseless rift.

    There is a certain mystic hour
    When pyramid and clay-tip grow
       Alive with darker power;
A mood unknown to Nature, a mortal mood
Caught up into His Godhead: taste of blood,
Anguish that makes each tip-frame a gibbet, bared
Until I feel on each the swing of my hand, a pale
Ghost-self of primal guilt that drives the nail.
And the Sphinx-mood is mercy, Olympus tame compared
With my deserts. Then I begin to know
       Why I am tested so.

A KINDRED BATTLEFIELD

(TO T. F. POWYS)

Thunder of swinish gods
    And the noontide heat too fierce
Upon the Chaldon clods:
    Yet calmly your eyes pierce

The gross, dank earth and cloud,
    The moody God's disguise,
Wherein His Cross has bowed
    The festering pagan skies.

Wounds in both God and swine!
    The strife of healing breaks
The passive hills that pine,
    The sullen sea that wakes.

White cliffs and goring hail!
    You watch the mystic tide
Lash where no prayers avail
    While soul and sense divide:

Soul seeking the Fatherland
    Beyond the heaven that frowns;
Sense brooding where it scanned
    Dead bones on Chaldon Downs.

This is the battlefield,
    Fluid and undefined:
Land, sea, life, death, revealed,
    Confused within the mind.

A labyrinth, a maze,
    Each chalky Dorset lane:
No landmark steadfast stays
    To guide the questing brain.

The baffling hedge of thorns,
    The swirling mist and sea,
The goblin world that scorns,
    Fret you continually.

Till noontide thunders cease
    And you behold the sign:
Buds potent with release,
    Promise of God's good wine.

Strength for the weary feet:
    Vision of inland heights.
The striving gods retreat;
    You find new paths, new lights.

The homely Stour may tame
    Terrors of Madder Hill,
The new earth name the Name –
    My clay-world feel the thrill.

Chalk heart and clay heart share
    A wilful strategy:
The strife you learned to bear
    Breaks westward over me.

THE TWO BEDS

(TO D. H. LAWRENCE)

You were a child of the black pit,
The grimy tunnellings where fuel and treasure
Are one, and yield to the shrewd blow,
And the stifling air awaits the chance gesture
Which brings the tension, flame and death
In the explosive blast; and the image
Remained with you, a blindness of those deeps
And strange distortions in the hot fumes
Too near the earth's bowels. You never saw
The clay as I have seen it, high
On the bare hills, the little breasts
So white in the sun, all the veins running white
Down to the broad womb with its scars.
And the scars meant, beyond fertility,
Purgation – symbol of the stained rock,
And the live water searching, cooling
Along the bare sinew; and then the heat,
The brief heat beyond the body; and at last
The cup for the new wine. (But that is yonder
And this is faith.) So I had the open view,
While you groped in cramped seams, found no heavenly
    clue.

But you sought always: all around the world
The one mind bored in the narrow duct,
Straining and twisting for the light, the other warmth
That comes with Springtide of belief, deep, deep,
In plenitude more potent than mere soul.

47

Could light of my clay have fallen
On your black pit (yet not my light,
But the Light that is not as you supposed;
I tell you, the Man who died
Is not as you supposed), why, then
Your symbol would have changed, flesh have been known
As clay-bed and not coal-bed, its yield
The patterned cup for the great Marriage-feast,
No brute-lump of dusky fuel, soiling, corroding
With its primordial stain as it goes unpurged
From the subterranean womb to fires of perdition.

You did not find the true flesh,
Which feeds no fire, though it is tempered
By fires of the Spirit, and does not lapse or swoon
In quest or consummation, nor taste oblivion
In love or death; it knows only
Life more abundant, which means consciousness
Ascending to the All-conscious, finding otherness
In vigour of the new Day, not slipping, gliding,
Fading down the shaft of drugged sense to the dead
Coal-forests where the dark gods reign, silently breeding
The sensual theosophy, the second death.

THORN IN THE FLESH
(TO SØREN KIERKEGAARD)

No desperate clutch
At normal growth can succour such
As Nature seals with this peculiar mark:
The twisted thorn that points towards the dark

And draws the spirit's sap
To its demonic congress and its flower
Of foaming and tormenting power.
And though we may
Resist the fated trap,
Protest and pray
To all the gods our thorn-warped souls divine,
We see no sign
And find no room:
Theirs is the kingdom of our doom.

And yet a miracle took place: you stood
In true beatitude
Free of the thorn-shade and the festering scum,
Into the other Kingdom come,
To the other God, the other thorn
From which the existential Moment leaps
In wilful scorn
Of natural deeps,
And breaks the destined pattern of the life
Which has appealed by faith beyond its temporal strife.

But there's a shadow still: Kierkegaard, you missed
The highest pinnacle of privilege where
The faithful flesh casts out the soul's despair,
And rapturously the living lips are kissed
To mark the rout of Nature. Had you but believed,
You would have seen your sum of life retrieved,
Fate driven from its last stronghold in the flesh.
Though this was offered, not predestined in your case,
Christ's offers are as sure as His decrees
Where human faith responds. He sees

Just what we need to break the thorny mesh
To its last fibre in the hungering clay,
And quench with steadfast sun the fanged Auroral flare
That maddens in the thorn-shade. When His grace
Suffices, as for Paul, He does not bring
The offer of a thing
Earthly and fair,
And put within your grasp the lovely form.
Why did you turn
From gift of passionate norm,
Afraid to let its ardours burn
Down to the dark thorn roots
And quicken there the choicer nuptial fruits?

THE CLAY ALTAR

From leprous sand
The thorn had fumbled, barring my retreat
Past furnace fire and kiln steam to the pastures wanned
By the broad winter, yet still sweet
To loitering lovers' feet.
I was forced on, pressed only by His moods,
To these scarred uplands where He broods
In central sanity and absolute Being.
But suddenly a touch
Surprises me beyond the thorn-shade's clutch.
No pasture – just the clay-lights' glare
On knotted glacial slopes,
With bristling stacks below and thorn trees bare:
Yet she is there,
Taking my numbed hand as it gropes.

Let all that desperate fleeing
From every charm of youth be tempered now
With tethering candour of a manly vow,
Though still the gritty symbols stay.
My passion bears a tone
Which I alone
Was bred to by the closeness of the clay
And the long incarceration where the grey
Dunes were my brothers and the white pit breasts
My only glimpse, in symbol even,
Of woman's bounty, fleshly heaven.
So my purged heart attests.

Only within the Moment would I dare
Accept this hour
Amid the leprous sand, the thorn-shaft's blunted power.
Half fearfully I name the Name,
Praying even as we kiss:
"No natural mate is this:
It is another altar of the wild,
And still unlovely save for one bright flame
That burns and bares her as Thy flawful child."

THE BROADENING SPRING
(TO KARL BARTH)

My clay-world's cycle is complete at last:
The icy judgement on these Cornish Alps
Recedes from mind and spirit as from heart.

I greet the distant Alps whence Springtide comes
To credal regions far beyond my clay –
Springtide with judgement in another guise –
Through sinuous ducts and tunnellings oblique
That reach the hidden fount of faith once more.
The living fount! Alive with anger too,
Though sunrise floods the sky in answering stress
Of passion as the fervid waters move,
Intent on conquering for the Unknown God
The death too well known on the land too dear
For mitigation of the healing shocks.

Crisp gleam of vigour first at Safenwil
As tools of Luther, Kierkegaard excavate,
Drill under crust of fashionable thought,
Heave up the torpid heresies and probe,
With hands whose mastery shows the praying soul,
The narrow text that yields infinity,
The knotted currents at the fountain-head,
The Pauline affirmations – perilous deeps
Where labouring seekers track the Godhead still
Dynamic in disguise. The veiling thrust
Of waters common to the spirit's touch
Is potent here with elements unguessed,
Inscrutable within the shade of God.

Yet faith must dare and does dare, for the swell
Of sunrise on the hills is God's command.
Faith plunges with her dower of subtleties
And gropes at bedrock in her breathless quest,

Then rising blinded at a frontier's verge
Awaits the visible sundering, life from death,
Eternity from time, God from mankind,
As shown in symbol where the waters dash,
Spreading from Safenwil to Munster, Bonn,
Till Europe is again engulfed in strife
Of slimy error with the massive pounce
Of existential Truth. The fused and free
Life of the Moment quickens where it will
And meets the secret searching of the soul
Which craves the living darkness in the tide,
Incognito of judgement that redeems,
Till frontiers are dissolved, identity
Secured in resurrection of the dead.

The tide has reached me; all my clay is changed;
The bed and battleground of solitude
Lie thawed in fellowship; my symbols fade
In recognition of the Citadel.

EPILOGUE:

PRIEST OUT OF BONDAGE

Dark, mutinous land: I shared
Its moods through my dead youth, but I am spared
To wake and live and know it a husk and tetter
Which faith and sunrise peel from my soul.
I slip with every other fetter
The Cornish bond, for I must be whole

Within the eternal Moment, and have no root
In soil or race, in the annals
Of the Celt, or in the dubious channels
Whence idiosyncrasies and tensions shoot.

I rise, no longer dark,
No longer mutinous, and embark
On the journey outward, the escape
To air that is rid of superstition, to a pulse
That draws no heavy blood from the obscure
Cycles of savagery, the historic shape
Of atavism. I shed the lure
Of a dim mother-breast I have outgrown,
And while the Moment's hot fierce joys convulse
My heart I take the irrevocable step beyond
Loyalty to this dead land: no longer bone
Of my bone is its granite, nor flesh
Of my flesh its clay:
The bright blade of the Word severs the barbarous bond.

Christ calls from the tarred road and I must go,
Not as an exile, no,
Nor as one deprived, but as one
Moving to fulfilment, moving home
Out of the ancestral mesh,
Out of the bitter moorlands where my tears
Fell on the sullen bramble and the dun
Rock of the derelict years.
Heir of the Moment and the electing Way
Whence all my treasures come,
I tread in the newness of truth
Where dawn-flushed pylons trample the uncouth

Spells of the tribal night. And this dead land
Which bore and moulded me for a fate
Sour as its soil and hard with its hate
Smoulders and glowers behind the plucked brand
It will never regain or understand.

Frontier Signals

CLAY PEAK

My destiny is drawn
    Sharp as the prongs
Of a clay-tip against the dawn,
    Unsoftened by the larks' song.

Two gleaming fingers on the white snout,
    Grotesque above the clotted cone
Of carnal doubt:
    They are Dogma's radiant bone.

Heaven's sunrise on the iron blade,
    Signalling earth below:
What need of Nature's creeping shade?
    Truth is aloft and aglow.

I have climbed from the fickle land
    Up the rigid track,
And see, from my elected stand,
    Faith's dayspring surging back.

ALIEN GRAIN

Two worlds and yet one substance:
The grey sand of refuse, the yield
Of machines in a mauled pit,
And close to it,
Dwarfed on the spring-sunned field,
Brown glistening heaps of sea-sand, like a chance

Deposit of alien tides
That leave a far sea's fertilizing grain
To challenge dereliction's stain.
Wave-washed injection, the salt sand divides
The clay field from the fate of clay:
Harvest enriched by golden sand shall flout the grey.

If my world then be sand it need not
Be sand of the pit, the outcast
Scab of sterility, left to rot,
Ignoble. What though my past
Be clay-land folded in,
Shuttered by refuse from the inexorable
Scarred womb of mortal sin?
I have a soul, a field ever bared
To the Heaven of miracle,
Lying within the ancestral vomits, yet
Fresh with the tang of surf where seaweeds fret
Unblasted rock. Thus I am spared;
And to my gravelly land
Christ brings from margins of His sea
The golden treasure, spilling secretly –
His fertilizing sand.

GOONVEAN CLAYWORK FARM
(TO MY MOTHER)

Near the white gashed cliff where the orchard
Held its brave menaced fruit
You crouched and were tortured
By the clang on the thrusting rails,

Watching the iron lines encroach,
Hearing the clash of the buffers
That signalled my fate's approach,
The grimy burdens rumbling through the clay.
You knew how the young earth suffers
And the last harvest fails
In a flurry of sagging soot,
And the fertile faith is an oasis-field,
Hemmed in and peeled
By the blast. But you could pray.

In the sodden ditch beside the line
You wrestled for the healing sign,
Though the orchard had gone,
Cleft through by the blundering blast.
The sweet fruits had gone, and at last
The old home fell to the stroke:
Its grey walls rocked and broke,
And we were left alone.

Stroke at the heart – and yet
There was still a mark of grace:
Though the orchard fell the stable stayed:
To this day it stands with its sweet warm straw,
The black trucks baulked ten yards away.
My desecrating fates invade
So far, no further. You overheard
By the scabbed cliff-face
Among the apple trees,
Only the fanged decrees
Of a derelict Fall
Whose gritty pressure did not daunt my seed at all.

For the stable spoke of an higher Law,
The birth of the Word
Who saw you when your fruit was mown
In the mire, and set
Bounds to the clay-waste, won
A new earth for your son.

RECLAIMED

The beams have been wrenched from the tip,
The rails torn from the slope,
And the sodden snout
Poised skyward seems more brutishly to mope:
Just a bald blunt pile in winter's grip;
Flood-waters rising as the dune sags
With dribble of slack sand, pout
Of loosened stone from crumbling rifts,
Where sleepers rot amid the drifts,
And at its mud-white base
The tangled wires are flicked
By the icy wind that nags
At the mass of scrap – old pulley-frames,
The waggon stiff and derelict,
Scarred signal-posts from the sunken face,
And the wooden gangway a girder mains.

I stand alone
On the dark rain-broken cone,
Rejoicing in a kindred nakedness.
My soul once felt the press

Of the iron track of fate,
The rumbling of the refuse-laden hours,
And the pitiless signals violate
My faith as the vomit spilled.
But now the fanged pit cowers;
Baptismal waters flood the bed of clay,
Fate's workings are stilled.
Storm-flesh of grace has bared my spirit's peak
And the scabrous flesh grows sleek
Till the young breast, immune and sealed
From fate, lies healed
In dreams of the reclaiming day.

BEYOND TRETHOSA CHAPEL

It flashed in Cornwall, at Meledor,
My rebel vision, kindling the scarp,
Cutting the bond at my spirit's core.
The Bethel stood in full view, a sharp
Alien scab across the dale,
On the fork of the hill: its lure was stale.
I had wrestled past it in my revolt,
And amid the sand-bruised furze
Was moulding my separate prophecy,
Climbing the ridge with my thunderbolt
To answer the worshippers.

But my hand is stayed; half guiltily
I shelter a hope of peace.
Beyond the gutted memory

Some heart may be ripe and rare,
Reaching to mine with a kindred stress,
Though she lets its flame be tempered – yes,
In the common house of prayer.

Mediate, then, beloved; let tension cease,
Dune-grit and pews be reconciled:
Let not the peak be cut away,
Nor the fold reviled.
Harsh clang of the prophetic tip
May yet be blent, through you,
With hymn of fellowship
My childhood knew.
Bless with your dreams my broken clay
As you take the broken bread;
Fuse the corporate flame with our lonely ray;
Show me that Bethel wine is red.

METEORITE

Faith has some blisses still
That striving flesh may name,
And in the recognition split the heavenly flame,
Receiving to its bed the meteorite
From planetary spaces of the spirit's flight,
Till the elected kiss
Reveals the clay-world oasis:
Sense nourished in the boundaries of grace,
The wayward meteorite grown precious in its place;
And challenging the carnal will
That once controlled our fates,
The cooled core dreams and mediates.

TREGERTHEN SHADOW

(TO D. H. LAWRENCE)

There was a day
When I slept unknowing, an infant here in Cornwall,
And you passed so near, your living breath
Terribly near me, and your shadow
Upon the unconscious seed for the brief touch,
The impress and delineation
Of its stain and flow within the fixed channel
Where yours had fretted and was rousing still,
Ablaze with potency. And the shade
Of your passing was marked by fate, and the mark stayed.

For there were times in after years
When I felt the vague stirring, the bruise
Of the dark unrest around Tregerthen.
It came up with the west wind
And with the amorous mists when the grey peaks
Of my clay-dumps sank to oblivion.
And I felt the chill fear
Lest your end should be mine and a strange god find in me
His way to Isis in her Cornish form, Isis
Of the grit-hard mystery,
Isis of the crag-clotted womb,
And my night-black pit become
A shrine where the unknown god might heal his wounds
In the intimate lapse.

This was my fate, I knew, unless the cleared veins
Of my clay were given back, and the clear skies
Showed the live mood, the untiring purgation

Breaking the natural channel, peeling
Your shadow from the slit cliff.
And the fog lifted, the wind changed course.
I was not deceived in my vision;
I was not for the Celtic Isis or the gods
Of your stricken shade, but for the Word
And white light on the breasts.

INTIMATE LANDSCAPE

Here is the holy ground,
Earth-womb where springs abound,
Some frank for my refreshment, laughing still
If clumsy hand disturb them, others numbed
To poison at an uncouth touch. I thrill,
Sensing these waters yet unplumbed,
Fearful that when I stoop to slake
My thirst I may mistake
Unless you guide and show
Which waters at which hours are mine to know.

Under a smoky sky I view white cones,
Some sharp with ice where fanged revulsions scab
Their bowels, while others mask the tones
Of smouldering volcanic heat;
Yet all are yours, and stab
Alike on casual lover's glance,
And paths along their slopes look similarly sweet
To one unlearned in subtly-hid significance.

66

Oh darling, lead me safely through the world:
Make clear each sign lest my male clay be hurled
To flame when it seeks cooling, or to ice
When lava leaps in you, hot veins entice
Beneath a white breast I misread,
Thinking it cold, and pass unconscious of your need.
Instruct my nerves in nuance of your smile
Lest clay-springs of your body deep and pure
Pulse out to consummating ardours while
I track dry kiln-beds, miss the lure,
And slink unpurged through stale dust-laden air,
Kiln-rafters darkening on my nuptial night's despair.

CLAY PHOENIX

Is this the end
Of my pilgrimage and battle – the enigma
Of lightning at noon, the quenched wires
On my peak of vision, the glum dunes festering
Amid smoke from pit-head fires?
I am far down in the pit, and blinded
By the ambiguous flash. Where the signals loomed
All is dark. Am I now entombed?

No, for I did not descend
A narrow shaft for my truth.
The bed is still broad, exposed to the changeful sky,
And there's a breeze among the cloisters
Where I grope for the unique transmuted vein
I saw once in the sunshine and shall find again.

I was right to seek that, the bedrock of nuptial sense,
For it is within the mystery inside,
Forever inside the world that lives in God.
The body too needs prophets in the winter,
For spirit's spring runs wild with flamy pledge
Of flesh beyond the mortal moment, the betrayal
And the dust where chastenings end.

Let my peak be smitten, then, I offer still
No sufferer's creed from a sealed gallery.
My soul foreknows its destined thrill
Beneath the ashes and the oncoming moon,
My phoenix-vision rising from the scorched heart.

I shall see the flesh that is clay, the open-cast mine
Where men are not trapped but work with the wind on
    their faces
And the cold rain stings them away from the sterile
    swoon.
No pit-props there to sag with the weight of the ego;
No hot salacious smear on the white rib:
Only, when the vein is touched, the signal granted,
Comes the sharp snap of blast
As the agnostic rock is splintered and the barrier passed.

SHALLOW YIELD

Bronze idols amid the orthodox
White dunes, the earth-dump sags,
Drowsing aloft from labour's shocks
And the deep-yielding milky crags.

Each dwindling face is scabbed as the pit
Whence rats and rabbits creep through the ferns
In the moonlight, and the spiders knit.
The potter's hand has been dented:
Ritual of blood and soil returns
Where purgatorial questing died.

Men burrowed here but found no clay:
The earth was smitten, its crust
Peeled, and the fertile lip submerged,
But the soil remained unpurged:
The tools could only grind and flay
For the vomit of rust.

So is the spirit's broken ground
Cast back to natural usage where
It swells the ignoble mound
Of dank submission, querulous prayer
Denied some flash of credal bone
In which true yielding lies,
God lets blind instinct claim its own;
Faith's embryonic striving dies.

MAX GATE
(TO THOMAS HARDY)

No fiery wrestling sent
The scribble of hope's astonishment
Through the dark pines of Max Gate!
You laboured with the unwindowed word,
Blindly submissive, greyly passionate.

69

Yet I lingered, sensing the ache which spurred
The tired hand onward with its task;
The smouldering thought which dared not ask
For signs of love within the irony.
I know the mood – no more than mood with me –
When chilly apprehension stirs,
And the soul is driven out
From comfort to the wild heath where the furze
Is cruel in winter, stabbing to the veins
Whichever path is taken. It seemed much,
In the festered moment, that your pity grew
Articulate from the touch
Of the thorns, the fallen pine-leaves. But you drew
Back to the negative release,
The closed curtain and the folded doubt.

I found, besides my thorn, another Tree
In the waste-land; I saw the pains
Fate-rooted – no divine caprice,
But alien fangs which the bright grace
Stoops and destroys when the wanderer's face
Turns homeward and the Tree is recognized.

You missed redemption's paradox amid
Those pines; so I had to bid
Farewell to Max Gate, though its strong
And sombre shade lay long
Upon me, half congenial still.
There at your gate I had surmized
How far the Tree may cast its healing thrill
Behind the curtained guesswork, the fear-numbed will.

And in the twilight, looking back
In lapses on my frontier track,
I almost could conceive
That to blaspheme with tears is to believe.

DAYBREAK IN DORSET
(TO MONICA HUTCHINGS)

It is not my fate that brought me here,
Though this is Hardy's land;
I am beyond my fate's frontier,
And in the realm of grace expand,
Heart truant and confused
With the flooding mystery –
A land so fertile, yet not alien to me.

Was not my language mere
Curt crumbling jargon of mauled rock,
Or purgatorial fire and sundering shock?
Yet the crabbed text grows pale
And I read instead the living litany
Of virgin earth unbruised
Of winding tree-domed aisles of Blackmoor Vale.

Fate-ridden land, in Hardy's view,
Yet every mood I have glimpsed today
On Dorset's face, each passionate hue,
Puts my bleak fate away.

I have seen the moment's fret
When thundery rain half vexed the little Stour,
And then the smile's full play.
As clear sun poured on hills where the sheep fed
And through the thatch-warm villages I sped
Till summer stood serene,
Enfolding me in rich fulfilment, dower
Of Dorset's heart
My fancy long had set apart
In dream-distilled Mappowder.

And I have seen
Fair golden evening drowse on Bulbarrow Hill
And on grey arch and parapet
Of old Sturminster bridge; then, all too soon
Sherborne in twilight cloistered as the moon
In cool strong candour veered from Cranborne Chase.

And in each new discovery, each tumultuous thrill,
There was no place
For fear of shaping scourge, though Tess's frail
Sad ghost might haunt the mind.
I had left my fate behind:

There could be no betrayal
Save in the night of doubt; and stronger, louder
Than the slurred dubiety
Was the voice of faith's new day.

I am purged now
Even of my purgation: the furnace fires
Are hot in Cornwall, and cold is the sand,
But I take the gentler vow
To sun that ripens when the fierce flame tires.

I have shed the scabs of my hard destiny,
I have crossed the frontier, found a living land,
A vision more complete
Because of Dorset's yield, so magically sweet.

MODELLED IN PASSION WEEK

The wet cloth was folded back;
The unformed lump stood naked for her touch,
So vulnerable and piteous, each day
Through Holy Week. It bore the clutch
Of a creative spasm which has passed,
Leaving the modelled cast;
And now, at the Emmaus hour,
Tense with resurgent power,
I kneel before my image carved in clay.

Winds of the spirit played
Beyond the skilled sense: art's fire was folded back,
Focussed and feeding on my eyes and lips.
Each detail was melted and remade
In the impersonal crucible, held fast,
Transferred. The clay lump took my soul
From the flame at her finger-tips,

The terrible soft potency
Of female strength aroused, in full control
Of the image. And what of me?

So often the anguish of betrayal
When a hand stopped moulding and drove the nail;
But not this time, though the hand that shapes
Is a woman's again. I touch the plastic head,
Corpse-cold beneath the cloth, still damp
On its little gibbet of wood.
What matters it now, this stamp
Of a capricious force I used to dread?
The risen man escapes.

If death lurks in the fertile mood,
I have passed over it and kneel
At my faith's Emmaus, in the cool of Easter Day.
There is a tomb not far away,
Burst open to reveal
Fate's ultimate bonds outgrown and folded back.

LUNAR PENTECOST
(TO RENÉE MARTZ)

Scarred stillness of the brooding bone
    In the slow wash of lunar light:
Such was my ghostly kingdom, a dreamer's land
    Which the real heaven had to smite.

It smote with song – just a fire-flake
    That clove a crater in my clay:
God's jazz-drums seemed to thunder
    Where His lava broke away.

There's a roar in the lunar valley –
    No blast with hard rock thudding down:
This is faith's new vein, a molten joy
    Stinging the brooder's frown.

Grim ritual of the isolate self
    Is doomed now, for the flame laps on:
The beating jazz-fire mounts the white skull,
    Enfolds the credal skeleton.

Hot ragtime stains the austere track,
    Bubbles and burns among my glacial clues;
I shall not find the way back
    To the crag's lip and the wintry bruise.

A fire-flake has pierced my silence,
    And a tongue responds – too deep
To be greyly solemn, too sure
    Of heaven's glowing heart to let me sleep

With the sufferer's image, that cold fang
    Of lunar mystery. Now I feel
God's gay eruption is bedrock truth
    Our stoic solitudes conceal.

BEYOND LOURDES

(TO ST BERNADETTE)

I, too, have waded to mystic ground
Through icy waters; I felt the sharp stones
In my darkened channel, Bernadette.
White fangs leap forward to God's mountain face
From the nagged spirit and numb bones,
And a cleft seeths with contact. There's a shrine
Where nightmare yields to shepherding grace;
The brief fold is fenced amid wolfish snows.

A fang struck the rock, you saw the sign
At your wintry Lourdes, and healing flows
Still from your wounds; and yet
In my own pilgrimage I found
That a vision born of pain
Dissolves in morbid rain.

Faith has schooled me further, brought me round
To the secret you may have lost
Through your suffering: heaven's vivacity
In the child world lit by Pentecost.

Its signal burst through the sidewalk throng:
Staccato winds from an exotic sea
Fanned the target heart until it stirred
With ragtime fibre of the Word,
And the poised lips grew strong
For a contact that needs no pauper's garb
No anguish at river-bed, no barb
To fire the shepherding song.

76

Bernadette, on your bleak verge
You could scarcely dream
How a jazz-throb gives the ultimate purge;
How the Cross bends closer to the neon-gleam
Than to the grim grotto; how a soul unscarred
By mystic snow and border-stream
May flash the healthier vision, spangled and starred.

THE VEILED SITTER

(TO LIONEL MISKIN)

Uncanny though not quite dark,
This rigid hour in which I sit
Marooned and fog-bound on the familiar chair.
Outside the cottage the rain and grit
Push mud to the lanes, and I am sealed
For a distant gallery's glare.
In the world of culture, elegance,
My trapped and truant mood should yield
Its fire on canvas. When the stranger's glance
Unfolds the artist's idiom, seeks the stark
Truth of my face, will the flame break through?

I send clue after clue
Against the fog-belt: a sparkle, a flash
Embeds itself where a thought should dash,
Spinning to blaze for the painter's eye.
But the signals die

Within the binding cloud: only the lips may show
By a sultry pucker, a softened rift,
How strange and rare is the sitter's gift
You would mediate and bestow.

The snaky mist
Has tunnelled down from a past so grim,
A fate so drab, a painter could limn
With Hogarth-smirch, Picasso-twist,
Yet not belie the pervert brow,
The humped will in the twilight. And what now?
You paint a man reborn through creed.

Pile on flamboyant colour: show my soul
Retrieved from the dead grey mask!
Bring Van Gogh riot to the task:
No wistful half-tones or granite glooms
Transmit the winged control.

Its bold rough bubbly light you need
To catch my spirit, trace the swerve
Away from the ego's fumes
And the tense blackened nerve.
The faithful lines will glow
With the convert's passion: you'll create
A hint of something shattered, and that's my fate.

HOMELAND

Those battle-torn frontiers will never waken,
    Though sometimes, as evening tires,
We glimpse their gorse-sour slopes, wind-shaken
    Against nebulous pyres.

It is too late to search the sombre shrines,
    Too late to take the baffled view,
The dusty march, or to hope that fortitude refines
    In desert or cloister, clay-rift, or pew.

We have reached the brittle pass
    Where sweet surrender alone stands clear,
And God's judgment turns to jazz
    At the penitent's tear.

This is the homeland privilege:
    The ponderous quest, the sceptic's pang, are spent.
Our goal is gripped on a razor's edge –
    Christ's ragtime sacrament.